# MOSES

## Illustrated by Tony Morris

Brimax · Newmarket · England

Moses was tending sheep one day on the lower slopes of Horeb, the mountain of God, when he saw a bush on fire. As he watched the fire, he noticed that the flames did not burn the bush. Moses was afraid.

Then he heard a voice coming from the bush. Moses knew it was the voice of God. God told Moses that he wanted him to go to Egypt and rescue the Israelites, who were suffering as slaves there. God wanted Moses to lead them out of Egypt to a new land flowing with milk and honey.

Moses was afraid that the people would not follow him and that Pharaoh, King of Egypt, would not let the people go. God promised to help Moses. Moses travelled to Egypt with his family and on the way he met his brother Aaron whom God had sent to help him. When they reached Egypt, they spoke to the Israelite leaders and told them that God was going to rescue the people. Moses would then lead them to the promised land.

Then Moses spoke to the Pharaoh. "The Lord God of Israel says that you must free his people," said Moses. Pharaoh replied, "Who is this God? I do not know him. I will not let his people go."

Moses asked God for help. God said to Moses, "Pharaoh has refused to free my people. Go and strike the river Nile with your staff and all the water will be changed to blood. The fish will die and there will be no water to drink."

Moses did as God commanded. Still Pharaoh would not let the people go. Next God sent a plague of frogs, after that a plague of mosquitos, then a plague of flies. After each plague Pharaoh was asked to free the Israelites but still he refused. So God sent more plagues to persuade him to change his mind.

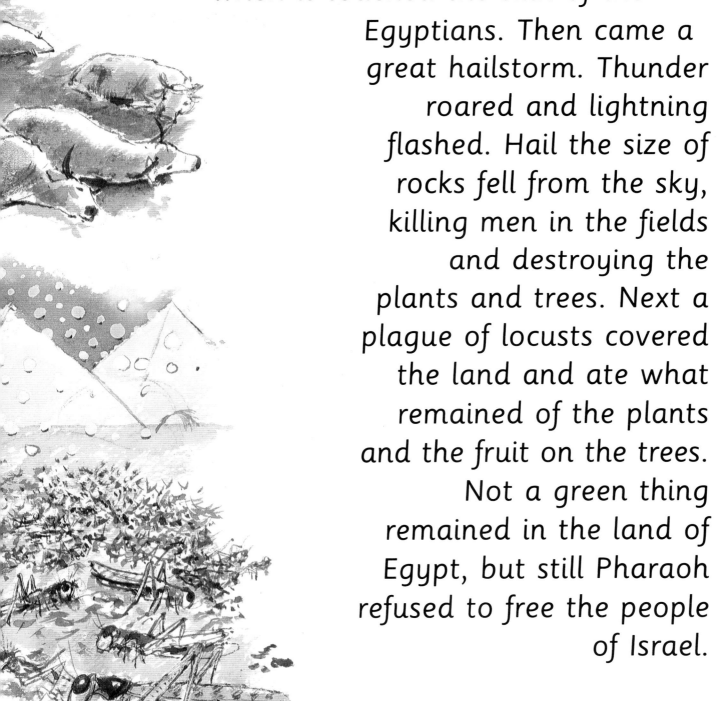

God sent a sickness which made all the animals die. Next he sent a plague of dust that turned to boils when it touched the skin of the Egyptians. Then came a great hailstorm. Thunder roared and lightning flashed. Hail the size of rocks fell from the sky, killing men in the fields and destroying the plants and trees. Next a plague of locusts covered the land and ate what remained of the plants and the fruit on the trees. Not a green thing remained in the land of Egypt, but still Pharaoh refused to free the people of Israel.

Then God said to Moses, "Stretch out your hand towards heaven that there may be darkness over the land." Moses did as God told him and the land was plunged into darkness. It was dark for three days.

Again Moses went to see Pharaoh. Pharaoh was very angry. "Get out and never let me see you again," he said to Moses. "I will never let your people go."

God sent one last plague down upon Egypt. He told Moses, "The people will be safe if they do as I tell you."

Moses spoke to the people and told them to listen carefully.

"Tonight," he said, "God's angel of death will pass through Egypt killing the eldest child in every family. To be safe you must kill a young lamb and spread its blood on the door of your house. The meat must be roasted and eaten tonight. You must all stay indoors. The blood on the doors of your houses will be a

sign to God that you are His people and He will not let the angel of death harm you. You must remember this night forever and celebrate it as the Passover feast — the time when the angel of death passed over your houses but killed the children of Egypt."

That night when the people of Israel heard the Egyptians cry out, they knew that God had done as he had said and had killed the eldest child in every Egyptian house.

Pharaoh sent for Moses and Aaron and told them to go and take the people with them.

At last the people were free and thousands followed Moses out of Egypt.

God showed Moses the way through the desert by day with a pillar of cloud and by night with a pillar of fire. Soon they came to the Red Sea where they made camp.

When Pharaoh heard that all the people had left and there were no slaves to do the work, he ordered his army and six hundred chariots to follow the people and bring them back to slavery in Egypt.

When the people of Israel saw the army in the distance they were terrified. They were trapped between the Egyptian army on one side and the Red Sea on the other. Moses said, "Do not be afraid. God will save us."

God told Moses to hold his staff over the water. Moses did as he was told. A strong east wind blew up and made the sea bed dry land with great walls of water on either side. The pillar of cloud moved behind the people of Israel and in front of the Egyptians. The people of Israel were able to walk across the dry sea bed. They walked all night with the light from the pillar of fire to guide them.

The Egyptians followed.
As soon as all the people
of Israel were safely
across, God told Moses
to hold his staff over the
sea again.
Once again Moses did as
he was told. The great
walls of water collapsed
and the Egyptian army
and all their chariots
were covered by the sea.
Every man and beast
was drowned.
Moses and the people
were safe and gave
thanks to God who had
rescued them from the
Egyptians.

God provided both food and water for the people on their journey to Canaan, the promised land.
Water in stagnant pools was made safe to drink when God instructed Moses to throw a log into the water Another time water came out of dry rock when Moses struck the rocks with his staff.

God made bread rain down from heaven and quails covered the ground providing meat. But no one was allowed to gather either meat or bread on the seventh day, which was the day of rest called the Sabbath.

Three months later they reached the foot of Mount Sinai and made camp. This was where God had told Moses to go to Egypt, free the people and lead them to the promised land. Moses climbed the mountain to speak to God. God told Moses to tell the people that as long as they obeyed him and kept his laws he would always look after them.

God said that he would speak to the people on the morning of the third day. Moses told the people what God had said.

On the morning of the third day, the mountain shook and was covered with smoke and fire. Moses spoke and God answered him in thunder and told him to come again to the top of the mountain.

Moses climbed to the top of the mountain and God spoke of the laws which all must obey.

These laws were the Ten Commandments.

| | |
|---|---|
| YOU MUST NOT WORSHIP OTHER GODS | *The First Commandment*<br><br>God said, "I am the Lord your God. You shall have no other God but me." |
| YOU MUST NOT MAKE IMAGES TO WORSHIP | *The Second Commandment*<br><br>You must not worship statues or pictures. Only God himself. |
| YOU MUST NOT TAKE GOD'S NAME IN VAIN | *The Third Commandment*<br><br>You must not swear using the name of God. You must not use God's name in disrespectful way. |
| YOU MUST KEEP THE SABBATH DAY HOLY | *The Fourth Commandment*<br><br>This means that we can work for six days but the seventh day, the Sabbath day, must be a day of rest.<br><br>God himself created the world in six days and on the seventh day he rested<br><br>God intended the seventh day for worshipping him. |

| | |
|---|---|
| YOU MUST RESPECT YOUR FATHER AND MOTHER | *The Fifth Commandment*<br><br>This means that you must listen to your parents and care for them. |
| YOU MUST NOT KILL | *The Sixth Commandment*<br><br>It is wrong to murder. |
| YOU MUST NOT COMMIT ADULTERY | *The Seventh Commandment*<br><br>When a man and woman marry they promise to stay together and be faithful to one another. This commandment means being loyal to the one you love. |
| YOU MUST NOT STEAL | *The Eighth Commandment*<br><br>It is wrong to take something that is not yours. |
| YOU MUST NOT TELL LIES | *The Ninth Commandment*<br><br>It is wrong to tell lies. |
| YOU MUST NOT COVET | *The Tenth Commandment*<br><br>To covet means to want something that is not yours. It is wrong to be jealous of another person and to want what belongs to them. |

God gave Moses more laws to
guide the people. These laws show
the people how they must love God
and teach their children to love
God and one another.
God gave Moses the
Ten Commandments
written on tablets of
stone.